THOMAS PAINE'S
COMMON SENSE

By Ryan Nagelhout

Gareth Stevens
Publishing

Please visit our website, www.garethstevens.com. For a free color catalog of all our high-quality books, call toll free 1-800-542-2595 or fax 1-877-542-2596.

Library of Congress Cataloging-in-Publication Data

Nagelhout, Ryan.
Thomas Paine's Common Sense / by Ryan Nagelhout.
  p. cm. — (Documents that shaped America)
Includes index.
ISBN 978-1-4339-9014-4 (pbk.)
ISBN 978-1-4339-9015-1 (6-pack)
ISBN 978-1-4339-9013-7 (library binding)
1. Paine, Thomas, — 1737-1809. — Common sense — Adaptations. 2. United States — Politics and government — 1775-1783 — Juvenile literature. 3. Political science — History — 18th century — Juvenile literature. I. Nagelhout, Ryan. II. Title.
E211.P153 N34 2014
973.3—d23

First Edition

Published in 2014 by
Gareth Stevens Publishing
111 East 14th Street, Suite 349
New York, NY 10003

Designer: Sarah Liddell
Editor: Therese Shea

Photo credits: Cover, p. 1 Louis S. Glanzman/Contributor/National Geographic/ Getty Images; p. 5 photo courtesy of Wikimedia Commons, Commonsense.jpg; pp. 6, 20 MPI/Stringer/Archive Photos/Getty Images; pp. 7, 19 DEA PICTURE LIBRARY/ Contributor/De Agostini/Getty Images; p. 9 Universal Images Group/Contributor/ Universal Images Group/Getty Images; p. 10 George F. Mobley/Contributor/National Geographic/Getty Images; p. 11 FPG/Taxi/Getty Images; p. 12 photo courtesy of Wikimedia Commons, Magna Carta.jpg; p. 13 Time Life Pictures/Contributor/Time & Life Pictures/Getty Images; p. 14 Stock Montage/Contributor/Archive Photos/ Getty Images; p. 15 T. Rowlandson and A.C. Pugin/The Bridgeman Art Library/ Getty Images; p. 16 John Parrot/Stocktrek Images/Getty Images; p. 17 Hulton Archive/ Handout/Hulton Archive/Getty Images; p. 21 David Freund/Stockbyte/Getty Images; p. 23 Hulton Archive/Staff/Hulton Archive/Getty Images; pp. 24, 25 Visions of America/Contributor/Universal Images Group/Getty Images; p. 26 photo courtesy of Wikimedia Commons, PaineAmericanCrisis.jpg; p. 27 Education Images/UIG/Universal ImagesGroup/Getty Images; p. 28 Francis Miller Contributor/Time & Life Pictures/ Getty Images; p. 29 A. Easton/The Bridgeman Art Library/Getty Images.

Printed in the United States of America

CPSIA compliance information: Batch #CS13GS: For further information contact Gareth Stevens, New York, New York at 1-800-542-2595.

CONTENTS

A Bold Idea 4

A Man of Many Jobs 6

It's Just *Common Sense* 8

A Necessary Evil 12

Kings and Rich Men 14

Honest Men and Ruffians 16

Accepting the Challenge 18

The New Government 22

American Potential 24

The Crisis 26

A Life of Purpose 28

Glossary 30

For More Information 31

Index 32

Words in the glossary appear in **bold** type the first time they are used in the text.

A BOLD IDEA

Between Thomas Paine's birth in 1737 and his death in 1809, the Western world saw remarkable political change. The United States of America sprang from the British colonies, and soon after, France underwent a revolution. Many of these changes were sparked by the tip of Thomas Paine's pen.

With the British colonies in North America in open rebellion against the British crown, Paine wrote a **pamphlet** called *Common Sense*. Published January 10, 1776, it rejected calls for compromise between the colonists and King George III, and declared the only proper action was to break ties with England. Paine boldly stated that the colonies should be free. The pamphlet was a sensation in the colonies, turning much of the population in favor of revolution.

It's a Fact!

Thomas Paine almost gave *Common Sense* the title *Plain Truth*.

COMMON SENSE

ADDRESSED TO THE *W. Hamilton*

INHABITANTS

OF

AMERICA,

On the following interesting

SUBJECTS.

I. Of the Origin and Design of Government in general, with concise Remarks on the English Constitution.

II. Of Monarchy and Hereditary Succession.

III. Thoughts on the present State of American Affairs.

IV. Of the present Ability of America, with some miscellaneous Reflections.

POPULAR PAMPHLET

Common Sense is believed to be the most popular writing ever sold in colonial America. Paine himself estimated that 120,000 copies were sold in the first 3 months after its publication, and some biographers think 500,000 copies were sold by 1783. The first printing sold out within days, and 19 American and seven British editions were printed. It was even translated into French during this time.

A MAN of MANY JOBS

Thomas Paine was born January 29, 1737, in Thetford, England. The son of a stay maker, he learned the skills of this trade from his father after leaving school at age 12. However, Paine worked a variety of jobs in England. At one point, he collected taxes. He was fired after writing a pamphlet demanding better pay for tax collectors, also known as excise officers.

Paine met Benjamin Franklin in London, England. Impressed by Paine, Franklin encouraged him to make the long voyage to the American colonies. Paine arrived on November 30, 1774. He became the editor of *Pennsylvania Magazine* in Philadelphia. His work as a colonial writer would make great waves soon after.

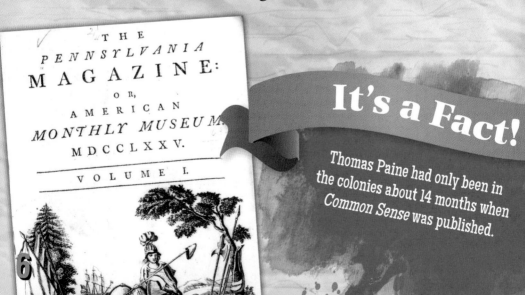

THE PENNSYLVANIA MAGAZINE: OR, AMERICAN MONTHLY MUSEUM. MDCCLXXV. VOLUME I.

It's a Fact!

Thomas Paine had only been in the colonies about 14 months when *Common Sense* was published.

Despite *Common Sense*'s popularity, Paine had many enemies.

CORSET CONSPIRACY!

Traditionally, a stay maker sewed corsets, a stiff type of women's underwear popular in the time of Thomas Paine. Paine's family lived in Thetford, a major shipbuilding center because of its abundance of wood. The stay makers there didn't make corsets—they sewed sails for boats. Still, many biographies of Paine call him a corset maker. The Thomas Paine National Historical Society says the rumor of his corset making was spread to make him seem less of a hero.

IT'S JUST COMMON SENSE

The American Revolution had already started by the time *Common Sense* was published. Battles had been fought at Lexington and Concord in Massachusetts in April 1775, and American troops had moved into British-controlled Canada. However, there was no official declaration of war, and many colonists were unsure independence from England was even wise.

Paine's *Common Sense* was published a few months after England's King George III made a speech to **Parliament** stating the colonies were in open rebellion against the crown. The independence movement in the colonies was becoming increasingly violent. Paine's *Common Sense* convinced many weary and uncertain colonists that separation from England was the only option. The pamphlet was bought—and read—in huge numbers.

It's a Fact!

Common Sense was first published anonymously, or without Paine's name on it. The pamphlet said it was "Written by an Englishman." Paine, like other colonists, still considered himself to be British.

Lexington and Concord were the first places that saw fighting in the American Revolution.

EASY READING

Part of what made *Common Sense* so successful was that it was easy for colonists to understand, even those without much education. Paine borrowed **philosophy** from many **Enlightenment** thinkers, but his style was his own. Instead of using Greek and Latin quotes or referring to ancient writings, Paine wrote in plain terms. He made many references to everyday life and used practical language that made it clear to most people.

9

Paine organized the pamphlet into four parts. He wrote in the first part about the origins of government. In the second section, he attacked the British monarchy and called attention to the unfair treatment of British citizens. Many **grievances** in *Common Sense* described wrongdoings in England. Having lived in England his entire life, Paine had more knowledge about that country than about the colonies. But the third section talked about the colonies in particular, arguing in favor of their own government and making suggestions about its organization.

The fourth and last section of *Common Sense* outlined the strengths of the colonies and demanded that a new colonial government declare independence with a formal **document**. Freedom from the crown, Paine wrote, was simply a matter of common sense.

Paine's writings helped many replace their fear of the British government with anger about its injustices.

It's a Fact!

Paine's family name was actually "Pain." He added the "e" when he moved to the colonies.

John Adams was the second president of the United States. Writing to his wife, Abigail, Adams said Paine was "a better hand at pulling down than building."

OUT OF ORDER

Founding Father John Adams described Paine as a man able to tear a house down, but lacking the skills to rebuild it. *Common Sense* was a bold argument against the traditional European social order of the 1700s. Even after the colonists had gained independence, Paine **advocated** for sharing wealth with the poor, ending slavery, and expanding women's rights. Some of these ideas were quite shocking at that time.

11

A NECESSARY EVIL

Society in every state is a blessing, but Government even in its best state, is but a necessary evil; in its worst state an intolerable one.

In the pamphlet's opening pages, Paine pointed out the differences between society and government. Society, he argued, exists because it's easier for people to live together than alone. A government should only exist to protect society from the evils of man. A monarchy, Paine said, doesn't do that. A proper government is elected by the people.

Paine discussed the "tyranny" of the British government, finding fault with the monarchy and the upper class. Paine argued that the common people should be represented in government, not lorded over by the rich and powerful.

← **Magna Carta**

It's a Fact!

In *Common Sense*, Paine called for a new kind of Magna Carta in the colonies—a "Continental **Charter**."

King John had a choice: sign the Magna Carta or face war with the barons. He chose to sign.

THE MAGNA CARTA

In 1215, a major change in British laws occurred when King John was forced to sign the Magna Carta. This document guaranteed barons certain rights while limiting the power of the king. It signaled an important shift in British government and is one of the documents that influenced the development of many **democratic** governments. However, Paine wasn't satisfied with the Magna Carta's impact on the British monarch. And to him, Parliament exercised another kind of mistreatment of the common people.

13

KINGS and RICH MEN

The nearer any government approaches to a republic, the less business there is for a king.

Much of *Common Sense* argued against the need for a king or queen in government. Paine not only believed that the colonies could operate without England and its monarchy, but that England didn't need a king either.

Paine made a case against constitutional monarchy, a type of government in which Parliament makes laws and a ruler enforces them. He thought this kind of government, which was favored by Enlightenment philosophers such as John Locke, limited the power of the ruler but didn't go far enough. To Paine, the common people would be better off without a monarch at all. He believed proper representation for most people was an elected government.

John Locke

It's a Fact!

Many phrases and ideas written by John Locke and Thomas Paine are found in other key American documents.

In his writings. Thomas Paine stressed that all men are born equal.

Parliament

JOHN LOCKE

Paine disagreed with John Locke about constitutional monarchy, but Locke's philosophy had an impact on the United States. Locke believed all men had natural rights, including life, liberty, and property. Thomas Jefferson used a similar idea in the Declaration of Independence and included "life, liberty, and the pursuit of happiness" as unquestioned rights. Locke also described a "social contract" people agree to when they create a government, thoughts echoed by Paine in *Common Sense*.

HONEST MEN and RUFFIANS

*Of more worth is one honest man to society and in the sight of God, than all the crowned **ruffians** that ever lived.*

Paine stated that powerful rulers caused wars. "In short," he wrote, "monarchy and **succession** have laid (not this or that kingdom only) but the world in blood and ashes." He argued a representative government would only fight wars believed necessary by the people. **Citing** examples from history and the Bible, Paine explained in plain terms the problems kings bring their people.

While Paine wanted less unnecessary war, he was far from nonviolent. The heart of his argument in *Common Sense* is that the colonies must unite and win a war against England to gain independence.

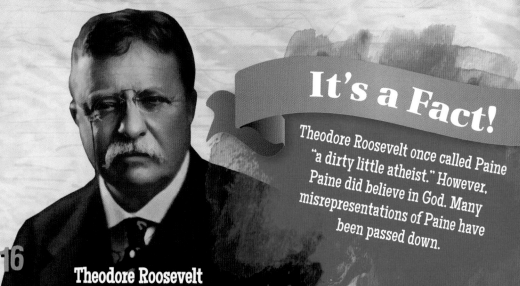

It's a Fact!

Theodore Roosevelt once called Paine "a dirty little atheist." However, Paine did believe in God. Many misrepresentations of Paine have been passed down.

Theodore Roosevelt

QUAKER ROOTS

Paine's father was a Quaker, a kind of Christian committed to nonviolence. As a result, Paine had a good knowledge of the Bible and used stories found in it throughout *Common Sense*. Paine's religious references stressed that all men were created equal, which he thought rejected the very idea of kings. Later in life, he had a falling out with the Quaker church and was refused burial in a Quaker cemetery when he died.

Paine had a falling out with Quakers later in life, but religion influenced much of his writing.

Quaker assembly

ACCEPTING the CHALLENGE

Arms, as the last resource, decide the contest; the appeal was the choice of the king, and the continent hath accepted the challenge.

Paine started the third section of *Common Sense* by stating there was only one choice for the colonists: fight for independence. "I offer nothing more than simple facts, plain arguments, and common sense," Paine wrote. He said the "period of **debate**" was over.

Paine went on to argue against the belief that England and its troops had defended the colonies in the past. He explained troops weren't used to protect colonists from "our enemies on our account, but from her [England's] enemies on her own account." Paine noted there were important differences between the interests of the colonies and the interests of England.

It's a Fact!

Taxes were imposed on the colonies to pay for the costly French and Indian War (1754–1763). Taxes were a major reason for the American independence movement.

England taxed paper, tea, and many products needed to live. Though many colonists felt the taxes were unfair, few could imagine an America without British involvement. The Boston Tea Party, a protest of the tea tax, is shown here.

WITH A FLOURISH

One of the most striking statements made in *Common Sense* is that the colonies would prosper without British involvement in America's economy. "America would have flourished as much, and probably much more, had no European power taken any notice of her," Paine wrote. He said the products made in the colonies could be sold to anyone and suggested they were held back by British trade limitations and taxes.

But Britain is the parent country, some say. Then the more shame upon her conduct.

Paine pointed out that the colonies had no interest in being enemies of countries such as France or Spain, despite their prior problems with England. Again, he distanced the actions of the crown from the goals and desires of those living in the American colonies. He once again accused England of not having the best interests of colonists in mind when governing.

Common Sense also stressed that the colonies needed to unite under common goals, though their desires were varied. Without a declaration of intent, Paine argued, it would be difficult for other nations to give the colonies help in their fight for independence.

Marquis de Lafayette, a French officer in the American Continental army

It's a Fact!

After the formal announcement of the colonies' independence, the Americans were aided by French troops, including the invaluable Marquis de Lafayette.

Many colonists rallied around Paine's pamphlet, crying for unity. The document even sparked local governments to write declarations of independence using language from *Common Sense*. Thomas Jefferson penned the official Declaration of Independence on behalf of all the colonies. It was adopted by the Second Continental Congress on July 4, 1776. Jefferson borrowed language and ideas from Enlightenment thinkers as well as Paine.

The official declaration Paine called for in *Common Sense* was published soon after his pamphlet.

21

The NEW GOVERNMENT

But where, some say, is the king of America?

Paine spent part of the third section of *Common Sense* describing a new government for the "United Colonies," as he named them. His proposal called for representatives from each colony to come together to write a "Continental Charter," an outline of a new governing body.

Paine wrote that each colony should send at least 30 delegates to this congress, which would meet each year and elect a president, not a king. A colony would be chosen at random each year, and a president would be picked from that colony. The congress was also charged with lawmaking. Three-fifths of the representatives would need to support a law in order for it to pass.

It's a Fact!

Paine wasn't invited to the Second Continental Congress, which formed the first US government.

Paine's proposed American government was very different from the one the other Founding Fathers decided to use.

THE ACTUAL GOVERNMENT

Despite Paine's plan for a new American government, today's three-branch structure (executive, legislative, and judicial) was what the Founding Fathers finally chose. Paine didn't support the legislative branch, a two-house Congress with a larger House of Representatives and a smaller Senate. He also thought the constitution should be rewritten at the will of the people. His ideas about women's rights and the abolition of slavery were also not applied in the new nation.

23

In the pamphlet's final section, Paine discussed the military possibilities of a colonial army. Citing the continent's natural resources, Paine described in detail the costs to build a navy that could compete with the powerful British naval forces. "No country on the globe is so happily situated, or so internally capable of raising a fleet as America," he wrote.

Paine said that declared independence was the only option for colonists and that England had chosen war with the colonies. He was confident this war was one the colonists could win. Soon after publishing *Common Sense*, Paine joined the army and helped fight for the cause he had so convincingly supported in his writings.

It's a Fact!

Paine is the only Founding Father not to have a proper burial site.

Paine served as an aide-de-camp, or assistant to a general, during the revolution.

THOMAS PAINE.
AUTHOR OF
"COMMON SENSE."
BORN IN ENGLAND JANUARY 29, 1737
DIED IN NEW YORK CITY JUNE 8, 1809.

VANISHING BONES

Paine was buried on his farm in New Rochelle, New York, but a decade later his body was dug up for reburial in England. William Cobbett, an admirer of Paine, wanted him to receive proper honors in England. The bones were lost, though, and today no one knows where they are. Some people claim to have one of his bones, while other bones may have been made into buttons and sold!

25

The CRISIS

After declaring independence, colonial soldiers struggled as they fought the mighty British forces. **Morale** was low in the colonies. Paine responded with a series of writings he called *The Crisis* (sometimes called *The American Crisis*). The first pamphlet, published on December 23, 1776, began with the now-famous line: "These are the times that try men's souls."

Paine's words helped rally the new Americans against the British troops. He published 16 pamphlets in all in the *Crisis* series, each without his real name and using the pen name of "Common Sense." General George Washington thought the first *Crisis* essay was so inspiring that he ordered it read aloud to troops at Valley Forge, Pennsylvania, during the brutal winter of 1776–1777.

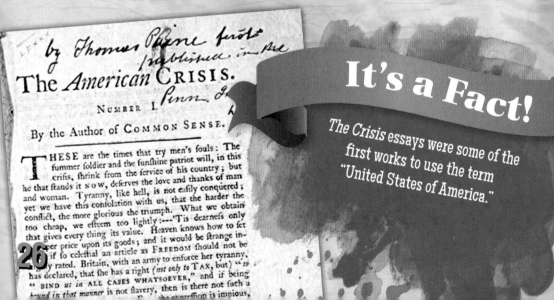

by Thomas Paine first published in Pd.

The American CRISIS.

NUMBER I. Penn. J.

By the Author of COMMON SENSE.

THESE are the times that try men's fouls: The fummer foldier and the funfhine patriot will, in this crifis, fhrink from the fervice of his country; but he that ftands it NOW, deferves the love and thanks of man and woman. Tyranny, like hell, is not eafily conquered; yet we have this confolation with us, that the harder the conflict, the more glorious the triumph. What we obtain too cheap, we efteem too lightly:—'Tis dearnefs only that gives every thing its value. Heaven knows how to fet a proper price upon its goods; and it would be ftrange indeed if fo celeftial an article as FREEDOM fhould not be highly rated. Britain, with an army to enforce her tyranny, has declared, that fhe has a right (*not only to* TAX, *but*) "*to* BIND *us in* ALL CASES WHATSOEVER," and if being bound in that manner is not flavery, then is there not fuch a

26

It's a Fact!

The *Crisis* essays were some of the first works to use the term "United States of America."

Common Sense and *The Crisis* weren't Paine's only influential works. During the 1790s, *The Rights of Man* was published in two parts as well as the first two parts of *The Age of Reason*. Both offered support for the French Revolution (1787–1799). Paine and his beliefs were viewed with some suspicion in France, though, and he even spent time in prison there. In 1802, he returned to America and lived the rest of his life near New York City.

General George Washington and his troops barely survived a tough winter at Valley Forge in 1776–1777. Paine's writing inspired them to soldier on.

A LIFE of PURPOSE

Thomas Paine was 37 when he traveled to America from England. By the time he died in 1809, at 72 years old, much of the nation had forgotten him. He spent his final days on his New York farm, a gift for his efforts during the revolution. Writing to a friend, Paine said he had a "life lived to some purpose."

Just about a dozen people attended his funeral, but over the years Paine's legacy grew. The bold document he wrote a little over a year after coming to the colonies helped shape the nation whose revolution inspires the development of democracy. Paine sparked a worldwide movement towards freedom in *Common Sense*, and it continues to change the world to this day.

It's a Fact!

Paine is said to have donated the money made from the sales of *Common Sense* to the Continental army.

TIMELINE OF THOMAS PAINE

1737
Born in England on January 29

1774
Travels to American colonies

1776
Publishes *Common Sense* and begins *The Crisis* essays

1791
Publishes *The Rights of Man* (part one)

1794
Publishes *The Age of Reason* (part one)

1807
Publishes *The Age of Reason* (part three)

1772
Writes *Case of the Officers of Excise*

1775
Becomes *Pennsylvania Magazine* editor

1783
Writes last *The Crisis* essay

1792
Publishes *The Rights of Man* (part two)

1796
Publishes *The Age of Reason* (part two)

1809
Dies in New Rochelle, New York, on June 8

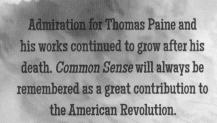

Admiration for Thomas Paine and his works continued to grow after his death. *Common Sense* will always be remembered as a great contribution to the American Revolution.

GLOSSARY

advocate: to speak in favor of

charter: a written statement describing the rights and responsibilities of a government and its citizens

cite: to mention something as an example to support an argument

debate: an argument or public discussion

democratic: describing a form of government in which all citizens participate

document: a formal piece of writing

Enlightenment: a movement that began in the eighteenth century and was marked by a focus on reason and a rejection of traditional social, religious, and political ideas

grievance: a complaint

morale: the mental and emotional condition of a group of people

pamphlet: a small book that gives information

Parliament: the lawmaking body of England

philosophy: a system of thought made to try to understand the nature of that which is real

republic: a form of government in which the people elect representatives who run the government

ruffian: someone who behaves in a rough or violent way

succession: the order or right of taking a throne or title after someone else

FOR MORE INFORMATION

BOOKS

Crompton, Samuel Willard. *Thomas Paine and the Fight for Liberty.* Philadelphia, PA: Chelsea House, 2006.

Vickers, Vikki J. *"My Pen and My Soul Have Ever Gone Together": Thomas Paine and the American Revolution.* New York, NY: Routledge, 2006.

Wilensky, Mark. *The Elementary Common Sense of Thomas Paine.* New York, NY: Savas Beaties, 2008.

WEBSITES

Common Sense by Thomas Paine
ushistory.org/paine/commonsense/singlehtml.htm
Read the pamphlet in full.

Thomas Paine National Historical Association
tpnha.keybrick.net
Become a member and learn all about Paine with this great online resource.

INDEX

Age of Reason, The 27, 29

American Revolution 8, 9, 20, 25, 26, 28, 29

colonies' interests 18, 20

Crisis, The 26, 27, 29

England's interests 18, 20

Enlightenment 9, 14, 21

equality 15, 17

freedom 4, 10, 28

independence 5, 8, 10, 11, 16, 18, 20, 21, 24, 26

King George III 4, 8

legacy 28, 29

Locke, John 14, 15

Magna Carta 12, 13

monarchy 10, 12, 13, 14, 15, 16

natural rights 15

necessary evil 12

new governing body 22, 23

parts of *Common Sense* 10

Pennsylvania Magazine 6, 29

popularity of *Common Sense* 4, 5, 8, 9, 28

religious influence 17

representative government 12, 14, 16, 22

republic 14

Rights of Man, The 27, 29

sharing wealth 11

slavery 11, 23

social contract 15

society 12, 16

stay maker 6, 7

taxes 6, 18, 19

women's rights 11, 23